"*David trained our team and we couldn't be happier. His insights, strategies and enthusiasm are simply amazing. He helped boost our morale and our revenue. If you have a chance to hire David to speak, take one of his courses or read one of his books, I highly recommend that you do.*"
—Steve Shattuck., Head of Americas Sales, HP

"*What a unique pleasure it is to watch David do his thing. It's exceptionally hard to keep people's attention, even in a short five-minute video lesson. And yet, from the moment you start to hear David speak, you're hooked. His energy, enthusiasm, and true passion for helping people comes through immediately, and you can't help but get locked into his observations. . . and what he's going to say next. If you haven't watched David in action, do yourself a favor and do so!*"
—Scott Milrad, Content Manager, Business Skills, LinkedIn Corporation

"*We have been waiting to work with David for some time now. The stars were aligned this year, and we were able to get him as the keynote speaker for our company convention. David blew the roof off the joint! His energy and enthusiasm are contagious, and he is an expert sales and customer service trainer. We signed up to work with him for the next 12 months.*"
—Shawn Fechter, VP Sales, EagleRider / Harley-Davidson Dealer Rentals

"David—YOU are the rockstar. Thank you so much for the incredible work you've done. People loved it and so we owe it to you for bringing the content to life for us. You were definitely overqualified for the job, so thank you for making time to do this for us. We must have you back for something soon."

—Wynnie Phipps, People+
Culture Leader, Oakley

"Thanks for coming yesterday. Your energy was amazing and contagious. I have had nothing but great feedback from the teams."

—Todd Hymel, CEO, Volcom

"David is a transformative speaker who has brought tremendous value to our company. With incredible knowledge and boundless energy, he has guided us on best practices in customer service and helped us find common ground and understanding as a diverse and inclusive workforce. David has been a treasure to our organization, and we look forward to having him work with us again for many years to come."

—Kelly Vlahakis-Hanks,
President & CEO, ECOS

CUSTOMER SERVICE SUCCESS

The 6 Keys to Deliver a World-Class Experience

DAVID BROWNLEE

Library of Congress Cataloging-in-Publication Data
Names: Brownlee, David, Author
Title: Customer Service Success: The 6 Keys to Deliver a World-Class Experience
LCCN 2021919729

ISBN 978-1-7368234-0-8 (Paperback) | ISBN 978-1-7368234-1-5 (eBook)
Business & Money, Marketing & Sales, Customer Service
Cover Design: 100 Covers
Interior Design: Formatted Books
The Brownlee Group LLC
San Diego

Note to the reader:

Congratulations! If you're reading this right now, you've probably made a decision to make more money through delivering superior customer service. You're in the right place. The bar is low but the competition is high, so you need to exceed your customer's expectations to increase your company's profits and make a positive difference; one customer at a time. This book will show you how. I'm excited to share some simple ways you can make large improvements to your customer service.

This book was written:

- in a conversational style to appeal to frontline workers, business owners, managers and executives;
- with exercises at the end of each chapter to provoke thought and practical application to your customer service delivery;
- in a layout that can be used with current employees as well as new hires;
- as a companion to our online, video and audio customer service and management courses.

I'll see you in the introduction.

—David Brownlee, CEO and Founder of
The Pure Customer Service Training Company

CONTENTS

INTRODUCTION

Welcome to *Customer Service Success*. Think of this book as a survival guide to navigate the new customer service landscape that we find ourselves in. I'm David Brownlee, international speaker, coach, and author. I'm CEO and founder of The Pure Customer Service Training Program and number one best-selling author of *Rockstar Service, Rockstar Profits*. I enjoy serving individuals in small businesses, executives at Fortune 500 companies, and everyone in between. Serving you is my passion, and I'm blessed to help transform lives every day. My mission is to help you find success, whatever that means to you, so you can grow your businesses or advance in your career. My goal is that the people I reach get more fulfillment from their professional and personal life and are able to spend time on what's really important to them.

What if there was a way to use customer service techniques to increase your revenues or your paycheck? What if there was a way to come to work every day excited and happy to be there? How do you create customer relationships so that your customers never want to leave? That's what we'll cover in this book. You'll learn why customer service is important, the role psychology plays in customer service, and how to truly understand your clients. You'll learn how to respond to upset customers and how to use empathy to overcome the challenges. Finally, you'll discover how to make sure your customer always leaves happy, so they will remain a client for life.

Let's jump in!

"If you are not taking care of your
customer, your competitor will."

—Bob Hooey

CHAPTER 1

WHY CUSTOMER SERVICE IS IMPORTANT

In this chapter, we're going to discuss why customer service is important—because it is! And it's super simple; it shouldn't be hard to provide excellent customer service. So, the question is: why is good customer service so hard to find nowadays? Think about a time when you had excellent customer service. Think about the experience. What did that person do? How was your interaction with that company? How did things go with that product or service?

Now, think about a customer service experience that wasn't so great. What went wrong? How did the person treat you? How did they make you feel? What happened with that product or service? Was it not working? Did you get it late? There is a huge distinction between companies that have great customer service and companies that don't. This is good news for companies wanting to improve revenue since shockingly few companies are intelligently looking at customer service as a key area to improve profits.

The first reason why customer service is so important is because it will help distinguish your business as better than others. Many products and services in an industry category are similar in quality. Let's take electronics, for example. Especially with all the big-box stores that are out there, the products are mostly similar in design. If you're looking to buy some sort of electronic item, different stores actually carry the same items, don't they? And, if they're really competitive, many of the stores also have very similar prices. With the similarity in products, and the similarity in price, what determines where customers go? Studies show that customers will choose the business with the best customer service if several businesses have the same items. In fact, nine out of ten customers say they would pay more to ensure a superior customer experience.

As an example of customer service affecting purchase habits, here is a firsthand account. When I had my anniversary, my wife and I wanted to go all out. We went to a hotel, and this hotel is awesome. I mean even from the time we first pulled in the valet, was asking our names, greeting us, making us feel like rock stars, which was fantastic. And the valet walked us into the hotel and at the front desk they said, "Hey, we've been waiting for you, Mr. Brownlee." And this particular time was my anniversary, and they let me know they knew this. They said, "Happy Anniversary." I said, "Whoa! That's pretty cool!" And then the bellman comes, and he's walking with us, getting information from us, other things that they can use to help improve our stay. And when we get to the room, guess what was there waiting for us? Chocolates and flowers and a little card that said "Happy Anniversary". That's special. This hotel really distinguished itself. Going beyond what is expected is a great way for you to distinguish your business too. I paid quite a bit more for that hotel room, and it was worth every penny.

For my hotel experience, I knew I paid more, AND I was happy with this. This is the first reason customer service is so important. Customer service will help distinguish your business in a world where a lot of products and services are similar in quality and price. Studies show that customers will choose businesses with the best service when several businesses have the same items, and nine out of ten customers say they would pay more to ensure a superior customer experience.

Alright, let's slow down for a minute, so you can reflect on your own customer service world, then we'll see you in the next chapter, and we'll continue the training.

Reflections on YOUR customer service:

What are three reasons customer service is important to you?

Why is reason one important to you?

Why is reason two important to you?

Why is reason three important to you?

"In the world of Internet Customer Service,
it's important to remember your competitor
is only one mouse click away."

—Doug Warner

HOW ONLINE REVIEWS IMPACT YOUR BUSINESS

In this chapter, we're going to continue looking at why customer service is important. One of the reasons it's so important is that review websites are everywhere, aren't they? Review websites like TripAdvisor, Yelp and Google Reviews; they're all over the place, and they're more popular than ever.

I travel a lot. When I'm in a new city and I don't know where to go for dinner, I will go on one of my apps. I'll pull up a restaurant, and I'll look to see how many stars it has. I don't know about you, but if it has two stars in front of the restaurant, I don't go any further. That's it for me. Now, if I see something with four or five stars, I'll read a little bit deeper into that restaurant. That's how I do it. And that is how a lot of consumers start their search for any kind of products online. Consumers consult review sites before making buying decisions. That's big. Negative reviews can keep customers from even trying your business in the first place.

On the flip side of negative notes, positive reviews can boost the number of new customers that contact you. Because reviews sites are everywhere, they're also very SEO friendly. SEO stands for Search Engine Optimization. What does that mean? It means the site will show up in search engines like Google, Bing, and Yahoo, and a lot of times, the review websites will show up even higher than the same business' website itself. That's huge. That can be the first thing your new potential customer sees about your business, so it's super important that online reviews of your business are strong.

I'll give you an example. A buddy of mine was getting married a few years ago in Playa Del Carmen, Mexico. Playa Del Carmen is beautiful—it's got the white sand beaches, it's got the palm trees, eighty-degree weather, crystal clear aqua blue water—it's absolutely amazing. Just being in that atmosphere feels like you're on vacation. And there's one main strip where there're probably hundreds of restaurants. We're walking along trying to pick one, but we couldn't figure out which one to pick. And we saw one that looked really good, and we're like, "Oh, this looks like a nice place." Well, hold on, let's go on our app and see. We went on one of the international review apps and looked up that restaurant. It had two stars. We ran away from that restaurant. We looked through the app and found another restaurant that had five stars. We ended up going to that restaurant and guess what? It was awesome.

If you want to increase your customer service experience, just go out in the real world, start using some of these apps, and start getting used to how they work, if you don't already do it. Then it is important to identify what businesses are doing that works and what doesn't. After making any customer service changes needed to be better, encourage happy customers to review your business. We already know that customers are using review websites, so you need to monitor what is displaying for your business and see how you can ensure that positivity is what people will see about your business rather than negative reviews that will scare them away. You want to help boost your customer service experience, and you want others to share the news as well.

Okay, so let's review. Consumers consult review sites before making buying decisions. Negative reviews can keep potential customers from trying your business in the first place. Positive reviews can boost the number of new customers that contact you. Review sites are very SEO friendly, so that means they show up in search engines like Google, Bing and Yahoo. A lot of times those search engines—those review websites—are even more highly ranked than your business' URL. Okay, make sure you get that: review websites are everywhere! They're super important, so don't forget to pay attention to them.

Let's take a moment to think about this, then we'll catch you in the next chapter.

Reflections on YOUR customer service:

Look at your company's online reviews. If you've got less than five stars, you need to create specific actions to improve your reviews.

What are three ways online reviews can positively impact your business?

____

____

____

____

How can you use reason one to your advantage?

____

____

____

____

How can you use reason two to your advantage?

____

____

____

____

How can you use reason three to your advantage?

____

____

____

____

What are three ways online reviews can negatively impact your business?

____

____

____

____

What can you do about reason 1?

____

____

____

____

What can you do about reason 2?

____

____

____

____

What can you do about reason 3?

____

____

____

____

"Customers gift you employment, pay
your bills, and give you the opportunity
for advancement and recognition."

—David Brownlee

CHAPTER 3

HOW CUSTOMER SERVICE IMPACTS YOUR LIFE

In this chapter, we're continuing to look at why customer service is important. And this one's huge. It's pretty obvious, but customers allow your business to exist. Without customers, there's no business, right? I mean, that makes sense, but we have to really look at this, and we have to look at why. Because you want to connect with your brain and make sure that you understand that without customers, you're in a world of trouble. It's not always easy to appreciate customers, especially the difficult ones, is it? So, let's take a look at this.

First of all, customers provide you with employment. Think about that. They actually provide you with employment; they pay your salary. Those customers give you a job, and they give you the opportunity for job stability. They give you the opportunity for pay raises and advancement. Okay? That's big.

Number two, think about this for a second. Your customers, even the difficult ones, allow you to pay your bills. Whatever those bills are, your customers allow you to buy groceries, send your kids to school, make your mortgage payment, and afford your car payment.

Okay? You really have to connect the lifestyle that you have with your customers.

If your customers go away—even if one, two at a time—if you start losing customers, you could lose your job. You could lose your ability to pay your bills, buy your groceries, send your kids to school, et cetera. Okay? That's big. What do you need do? You need to make your customers feel special and appreciated, every day. Here's why: it's six to seven times more expensive to acquire a new customer than it is to keep a current one. I love this for business owners.

I talk to business owners all the time, and their focus is on sales and marketing, which is very, very important. But what they don't realize is if you get that marketing, your customer comes in, you do the sale, they buy your product, but if that customer goes away, it's six to seven times more expensive to replace that customer than just to keep that customer, by treating them right and keeping them happy. With this, you can sell to them again without spending all the extra marketing dollars. And, if they're happy, they'll go tell their friends; they'll give you a good review on a website. Okay? So, it's important to remember that keeping a customer is way cheaper than attracting an entirely new customer.

A few years back, I had to get internet put into my house. I had just bought a new house and wanted to get online as soon as I could. At that time, I had been working from home so this was huge for me. I really needed the internet access. What happened was that the company I selected scheduled the installation for a Monday, but Monday came and went—no internet. I called them up, and they said, "You know what? We're going to send somebody tomorrow." The next day, Tuesday, came and went. Nobody showed up. I'm a pretty nice guy, but I was getting upset, right? Wednesday same thing, came and went—nobody. Finally, by Friday somebody shows up and installs the internet. I'm pissed. I mean, if I didn't have a work order in already, I would have switched companies right there. Fast forward to the following week. You know, somebody calls and follows up and says, "Is everything alright?" I'm like, "Well, it's in there now, so I'm okay." We went through the call, and I let them know about my frustration at how long it took. Fast forward a couple more days. I get a knock on the door, and it's a delivery guy. He's got a box, and he says, "This is for you, Mr. Brownlee." I open the box. Guess what's inside? A box of cookies from this cable provider that said, "Mr. Brownlee, we're so sorry for the delay. We screwed up; please accept our apologies and these cookies."

Whoa! That was pretty cool—an apology and cookies. That made me feel special and appreciated. They screwed up. And, by the way, is that going to happen in your business? Are you guys going to screw up? Is your company going to screw up? Are your coworkers going to screw up? The answer is yes. Here's the important piece: if you do screw up, you have to go above and beyond to make your customer feel good again. That is exactly what this company did for me. I would have avoided using them in the future because of a mistake they made, but they kept me as a customer by owning the mistake and making me feel they understood and cared about me.

Here's a ninja secret. You guys want the ninja secret? If you have an upset customer, and you can turn them around and make them a happy customer, that customer will never leave you. Why? Because they've put so much emotion into that transaction. Even if it's a negative emotion, there's so much emotion in there, you guys are together, and as long as you are able to turn the negative experience into a positive emotion, you've got that customer on your side. Have you ever met anybody who is maybe in a bad relationship that they should have been out of a long time ago? Why are they still together? It's that emotion; even a negative emotion can keep you in there. What you want to do is take that negative emotion and flip it over to a positive emotion. And that's going to create a loyal customer.

Let's review quickly. Customers provide you with employment and the opportunity for job stability, pay raises, and advancement. Customers allow you to pay your bills, buy groceries, send your kids to school, et cetera. And you need to make your customers feel special and appreciated every day because it's six to seven times more expensive to acquire a new customer than it is to keep a current one.

Reflections on YOUR customer service:

What are you most thankful for from your customers?

____

____

____

What are three ways you can show appreciation to your customers (either to reward a loyal customer or to apologize for a poor customer experience with your company)?

____

____

____

How will the first way make your customer feel appreciated?

____

____

____

How will the second way make your customer feel appreciated?

____

____

____

How will the third way make your customer feel appreciated?

____

____

____

"Psychology is the mental characteristics
or attitude of a person or group."

–Oxford Dictionary

CHAPTER 4

THE ROLE PSYCHOLOGY PLAYS IN CUSTOMER SERVICE

In this chapter, we're going to take a look at how psychology plays a role in customer service. What is the psychology of customer service? And we're going to look at it from three different parts. In this chapter, we're going to look at it from the psychology of your company, and in upcoming chapters, we'll look at the psychology of your customers, and the psychology of you. Okay, let's get going.

Let's start with the psychology of your company. First of all, your company values and mission must be in alignment with the policies and procedures for your customer service. I'll say that again: your company values and mission must be in alignment with the policies and procedures of your customer service. What does that mean? If you have, in your mission statement, that your core values are to provide excellent customer service, your system needs to allow and empower your customer service representatives (or your front-facing staff) who are interacting with your customers to take care of your customers. They need to be empowered to take care of the customers in the right way. Whether it's refund policies, whether it's flexibility or discounts, or anything like that, it really needs to be geared to help the customer. This helps the business as well, obviously, but the focus really needs to be on the customer.

Number two: management must lead by example in customer service. Okay? And especially with communication. It is important to get buy-in from the staff and team members on customer experience practices. When you have a manager, and you have staff below them, the staff are looking to the manager for cues on how to behave, cues on how to handle customers, and cues on how to communicate with each other—the internal customer, right? The people who you work with are your internal customers. How are you communicating with them, as well as your external customers? And here's what I see time and time again: I'll go into a company, and I can tell right away why the customer service is suffering—because the management is not setting the right example. Does that make sense? Business directors, managers, and frontline employees have to be in alignment for a company to truly possess a consistently positive customer experience standard.

Number three: if the company and management are not working with integrity in their core values and mission statement, a common vision of customer service will be missed. Most companies have stated values and a mission. And, by the way, if you're in a company that doesn't have stated values and mission, create something right away! Put together three to five core values that your company is going to stand for. That's going to help you make your decisions in putting together your customer service system.

You have to have integrity with your company values and mission and then the positive effects will trickle down to your customers. Counter to this, if you are lacking in a written company values and mission statement, and there is inconsistency in management, the negative effects, if you're not in alignment, will trickle down to the customers as well. Your customers are going to feel it if your company doesn't have integrity or is even simply out of alignment.

When you look at the core values and mission of the company you own or work for, you want to make sure that your own personal values and mission are in alignment with that company. You want to make sure that, hey, your company is not over here and your values are over there, because the customer is in the middle, and you'll never be able to connect those dots. You want to make sure that they are in alignment. Okay?

To summarize, company values and mission must be in alignment with policies and procedures, and management must lead by example in customer service and communication to get buy-in from staff and team members. Because if the team members watch the management treating the customers like crap, where is their motivation to treat the customers with respect? And if the company and management is not running with integrity, values, and mission, then the negative effects will trickle down to the customers. We're going to look at some more ways that psychology influences not only just the company, but also your customers and yourself in the following chapters.

Reflections on YOUR customer service:

Does your company have a written mission statement, stated values, and customer service policy?

If so, just to remind yourself of it, write your company mission statement here:

____

____

____

____

Also, if you do not have written company values and a customer service policy, I'd advise you to create this today (and you might be surprised at how rewarding creating this document can feel).

Is your company living up to its customer promise?

What are three specific actions you can take to ensure that you are living up to your company's customer service policy and customer promise?

____

____

____

____

How does action one show alignment with your company's values and mission?

____

____

____

____

How does action two show alignment with your company's values and mission?

____

____

____

____

How does action three show alignment with your company's values and mission?

____

____

____

____

"Customers are not always right,
but they always leave happy."

–DAVID BROWNLEE

CHAPTER 5

THE PSYCHOLOGY OF YOUR CUSTOMER

In this chapter, we're going to look at the psychology of your customers. Have you ever come across this before, where you're talking with a customer, and maybe they're an upset customer, and you're just trying to understand what they want? You're asking yourself, "What do our customers want from us? What is it they're trying to achieve?"

The good news is that your customers only want three things from you. Wait a minute, David, that's crazy; my customers only want three things? The answer is, yes. When it comes to psychology, your customers only want three things from you. And when you simplify what your customers want, it makes customer service a lot simpler.

The first thing your customers want from you is *they want to be heard*. Your customers want to be heard! They want to be heard all the time, but especially if they have a problem with your customer service, or your product, or if your service isn't what they expected or wanted, or something has gone wrong. As I've mentioned, things do go wrong, but when they do, you have to make sure your customers feel heard. Okay?

The second thing your customers want from you is *your customers want to be understood.* They want to be understood. You can even say things like, "Hey, I understand." That goes a long way! Because a lot of businesses today, you know, people aren't even listening to what their customers are saying to them. They're trying to formulate an answer and stick to a policy whether or not the customer is screwed and that's it. Right? Your customers want to be understood.

The third thing your customers want from you—there're only three things—is *your customer wants to be cared for.* They want to be cared for. Make your customers feel special, alright? We talked about that in the last chapter. What can you do to make your customers feel special and cared for?

There's a company, a shoe company; it's a huge shoe company. In fact, it's so big that they sell more than just shoes. But they've built this company—a multi-billion-dollar company—on customer service. And this is what I love because everything from the top down is based on how they are going to serve the customer. It gets so good with this company that if you're talking to a customer service rep and let's say you have a problem, they're still willing to talk with you, they're engaging you. Let's say you're going through something horrible, something not even related to the company's product. Let's say it is bad, like one of your pets died or something like that. The customer service agents of this company are empowered to the point that they can send you flowers and the company will pay for it. They'll send you flowers, and they'll write you a personal note—"Hey, I know you're going through a tough time. I hope you feel better."—whatever it is, and they can send that off to the customer. How cool is that?

It gets even better. This company has hired somebody, and their only job is to walk around the customer service floor, while customer service reps are on the phone, listening to what's going on. Let's say, for example, you are a customer, and you go on the company website and you want this particular item, but they're out of stock. The customer service representatives are empowered to go to a different website, from a completely different company, and purchase that product for you. You don't even have to purchase the product. They'll purchase it for you, they'll pay for the shipping, and they'll ship it to you. The person who goes around the floor is a supervisor whom the call agents have immediate access to, and this supervisor can make bold decisions on the spot. Is that cool or what? But you might be thinking, "David, that's a ton of money! Who can afford to do something like that?" Well, this is a multi-billion-dollar company but still, they're running a business. How did they do it? They took a piece of their marketing budget and instead of spending it on a Superbowl ad, they spent it on programs like this, programs where the customer feels cared for. Pretty cool, huh?

Ask yourself: what you can do in your company to make your customers feel cared for? Maybe you're not buying them items and shipping them things, but maybe you're writing a little personal note, just the cost of a stamp and a little piece of stationery, to send out to your customers to make them feel cared for. Often the small gestures can provide as much of an emotional boost to a customer as any expensive refund or other strategy would provide.

Okay, let's review. The psychology of your customers is they really only want three things. Your customers want to *be heard*, your customers want to *be understood*, and your customers want to *be cared for*.

Alright, let's focus on you for a minute, and then we'll catch you in the next chapter.

Reflections on YOUR customer service:

What are three specific actions you can take to make sure your customers feel heard, understood, and cared for?

____

____

____

____

____

Why would a customer want to feel heard?

____

____

____

____

____

Why would a customer want to feel understood?

____

____

____

____

____

Why would a customer want to feel cared for?

____

____

____

____

____

"If you are tuned out of your own emotions,
you will be poor at reading them in other people."

—DANIEL GOLEMAN

CHAPTER 6

YOUR PSYCHOLOGY AFFECTS YOUR CUSTOMER SERVICE

In this chapter we're continuing to discuss the psychology of customer service. We covered what the psychology of your company needs to be, what the psychology of your customers is like, and now we're going to look at the psychology of you.

I'll start with the first thing—the most important thing—you need to remember when you come to work every day. You need to come to work with a positive attitude. Isn't that true? If you want to deliver truly excellent customer service, and you want to create customer loyalty where that customer will never leave you, you need to have a positive attitude! Regardless of what else is going on in your life, because life happens, doesn't it? But, when we step in front of that customer, all that needs to go away. The only thing that's important is that customer.

When you have a positive attitude, you set the tone for a positive relationship. You set the tone for a positive transaction. If you have a negative attitude and you're frowning and standing slumped over with your arms crossed (even if you don't realize it), what message does that send? Or, if your client walks in and you're there with a nonchalant, careless attitude, and you're texting and look up at them: "I'll be with you when I'm done with this text. . ." What kind of message does that send? You need to have a positive attitude; one that says you're happy to see that person, and you want them to be there. That's the first thing.

The second thing is having a thankful mindset. Right? If you go back a few chapters, we highlighted that customers are your livelihood. Without customers, there's no business. You're not paying your bills; you're not getting those opportunities for advances and pay raises—that all goes away. You have to have that thankful mindset, and you have to tell your customers "thank you" every day. Every day, you should thank every single customer, even the upset customers. Because hopefully, with the customer service tools below, you'll be able to turn them around every time.

I love acronyms. The first customer service tool I'll highlight is an acronym: "Take a SEC." S-E-C, because it only takes a second to do. The first thing in SEC is smile. You have to smile. When you smile, it is hard to be angry. Do this while you're sitting there right now. Put a big smile on your face. If people are around, that's okay. If they're looking at you, just wave at them. Just put on a big smile. Now, try to get upset while you're smiling. Just really do it—you have to smile, but just get upset. See if you can do it. You can't do it, can you? Studies have put clinically depressed people in front of a mirror and had them smile for twenty minutes. The result was that during this activity of smiling, they couldn't get into depression. That is a big deal. Depression is a very serious thing in our country, isn't it? It's a very serious ailment. But the smile alone gets your endorphins going and it's contagious, isn't it? When you smile at somebody, don't they naturally smile back? Okay? Now, if there's an upset customer, you can only smile for so long or you'll get punched in the face. But if you start the transaction with a positive attitude, a thankful mindset, and a smile? I think you get the point.

Next, the E in SEC is eye contact. Make eye contact. Because if you are focused and have eye contact, that shows that you care for what they have to say. You're really trying to understand what they're trying to convey to you. When you make eye contact, you are more engaging than when somebody is talking to you and you're just kind of looking down, or even if you're looking towards them and you're just kind of not there, you're not present. Make eye contact and be present, so you can really listen. Later, we're going to give you some skills to work on that as well. Okay?

Next, the C in SEC is compliment or a comment. I love this stuff. A compliment: "Hey, I love that shirt!" or, "Hey, that's a nice necklace!" Or, you can comment on something: "It's hot out today, isn't it?" Whatever it is, a little compliment or a comment, that's going to build something called rapport—a commonality. It's where you start building a relationship, just as any other relationships you've built with friends or coworkers or anybody else. Okay? A compliment or a comment can go a long way. Your compliment might just get a slight nod of appreciation from someone already having a great day, or your small gesture might just be the day-changing inspiration someone needs to hear. This is not only wonderful for the recipient of the compliment, but it will create a lasting bond between them and your business as well.

I like Mexican food. Recently, I went to this Mexican food restaurant; it's pretty cool. It's not fast food, but it's not really a sit-down restaurant either. What you do is you enter a line and build your burrito or you build your salad or whatever it's going to be. You're in line and you're stepping down the way, kind of like a conveyer belt. There's a lady behind me and at one point, the person who was preparing her food looked up and said, "Hey, I like that shade of lipstick." She said it pretty loudly. I mean, everyone could hear it. But the lady with the lipstick next to me says, "Excuse me, what did you say?" And the worker repeated herself, "I really like that shade of lipstick on you." Instantly, I could see the joy in the lady behind me. A smile came on her face, she blushed a little bit, and she got so excited just from one little comment. I could tell it made her day. This little compliment could have made her week! Who knows what this lady was going through? Just one simple compliment was an act of kindness. Have you ever been having a bad day and somebody did some little act of kindness—maybe it was a stranger—and you just felt a little bit better? Little gestures like this really seem to put some faith back in humanity. Yeah, just a little bit of kindness goes a long way.

Let's review. You need to start with a positive attitude. A positive attitude is going to set the tone for any transaction and build a relationship between your customer and your business. Next, you want a thankful mindset. You want to tell all of your customers, "thank you" and be thinking with a thankful mindset. And next, Take a S-E-C— smile, eye contact, and compliment or comment. It is really that easy.

Okay, let's pause to think about your situation, and then let's get going in the next chapter.

Reflections on YOUR customer service:

What are three things you can do to make sure that you show up to work with a positive attitude toward your customers?

____

____

____

____

____

____

Why is smiling a great thing?

____

____

____

____

____

Why is making eye contact important?

____

____

____

____

What is one compliment you could use on a customer?

____

____

____

____

"The goal of a company is to have customer service that is not just the best but legendary."

–Sam Walton

CHAPTER 7

UNDERSTANDING YOUR CUSTOMERS

In this chapter, we're going to discuss understanding in customer service. Wouldn't it be great to really understand what your customers want? You have to understand what your customers want in order to provide excellent customer service. The first thing you have to do is ask intelligent questions. David, what do you mean? The best way to understand somebody is to ask questions. Have you ever heard of the eighty/twenty rule? Where you're talking twenty percent of the time and listening eighty percent of the time? This strategy is how the best leaders really transform and enact change—by listening and taking in information 80 percent of the time rather than talking 80 percent of the time as many A-type personalities are prone to do. This chapter we'll examine a few introductions and phrases that can assist in great customer service.

Customer service all starts with a greeting. It can be on the phone, it can be in person, it can be in an email, or it can be on a live chat. But always start with something like, "Thank you for choosing (your company). My name is David; how can I help you today?" Why do you say that? Starting with something like, "Thank you for choosing Pure Customer Service. My name is David; how can I help you today?" sets a tone with a positive attitude. And it includes a great question: "How can I help you?" It shows you want to know what it is that the customer needs. And I love the word "choosing." What does that presuppose? It presupposes that they've already chosen your business or service, right? "Thank you" is in tune with your thankful mindset. The first thing you say is "thank you." I didn't answer the phone and start with "Pure Customer Service." Or even better, these companies are out there, they answer the phone like this: "Hello." Is this a business? Um, what is this? That sets an entirely different tone of confusion, doesn't it? It also expresses a lack of professionalism. "Thank you for choosing Pure Customer Service. My name is David; how can I help you?" Okay, that is an easy formula to get the customer service interaction off to a good start.

After the initial introduction, depending on the situation, another good question might be phrased as, "So that I can take excellent care of you, can you tell me what happened?" If there's an upset customer, what am I telling them? I'm telling them that I'm here to take excellent care of them, and I'm interested in learning what their issue is, so I might be able to help solve it. And they're going to explain whatever the problem or issue that they're having is. "So that I can take excellent care of you, can you tell me what happened?" This is a great sentence because the customer, even before I offer to help, understands that I'm interested in taking excellent care of them. The customer knows that, in my mind, taking care of them is my first priority.

The next question, which is another good one to use with an upset customer is, "How can I make this right for you?" Or alternatively, "What can I do to fix this for you?" These can be two of the scariest sentences in customer service, right? Because you never know what the customer is going to say, especially if they're upset. And David, there's no way I can just ask them to tell me what to do! You can. And here's why: nine out of ten people who are upset and have a problem with your product or service, when you ask them the question, "How can I make this right for you?" or, "What can I do to fix this for you?" suddenly become sane again. Like, "Whoa, wow, this person actually cares about me; they actually understood what I was saying. This is good; they heard me." Okay?

Now some clients are going to say something outlandish and we're going to talk about what to do with that. It doesn't mean that you have to do what the customer says, but you ask the question. Most people will say something, and they'll give a recommendation for a remedy that's even less costly than what you would have recommended anyway. Your customers want to be heard, especially when they're upset. Ask intelligent questions: "Thank you for choosing Pure Customer Service. My name is David; how can I help you today?" Or, "So that I can take excellent care of you, can you tell me what happened?" Or "How can I make this right for you? What can I do to fix this for you?" All of these let your customer feel you're ready to listen to them.

As an example, in my company, whenever I do training or I'm going for a speaking engagement, I ask questions to my clients. I want to know exactly what it is they're looking for. And I repeat my questions to them, so I make sure that I understand exactly what they want. It matters less what I think the client wants to see from me than what the clients themselves want to see from me. By repeating questions, I can be confident about their exact expectations. I also learn if there's even a fit of whether I can deliver exactly what they're looking for or not. Does that make sense? Alright, I hope you take a look at the questions you want to use with your customers. I'll look for you in the next chapter.

Reflections on YOUR customer service:

What are three phrases you can use with your customers to make sure that you understand what they want and need?

____

____

____

____

____

How does the first phrase help you understand what they want?

____

____

____

____

____

How does the second phrase help you understand what they want?

____

____

____

____

____

How does the third phrase help you understand what they want?

____

____

____

____

____

"Most people do not listen with the intent to understand; they listen with the intent to reply."

–Stephen R. Covey

CHAPTER 8

CUSTOMER SERVICE: THE POWER OF LISTENING

In this chapter, we're going to discuss understanding your customers. In chapter seven, we showed that the first thing you have to do is ask your customers intelligent questions. The second thing you have to do if you really want to understand your customers is listen intently. You've asked them some intelligent questions. Now you have to listen. You want to listen to exactly what the customer wants, not what you want to hear, and take notes if necessary. Okay? When I have clients and I'm asking them questions, I'm listening to exactly what they're telling me. I'm also trying to make sure that I understand what they're telling me, so I can provide exactly what they need.

Here's a little trick. You guys want a little trick? This is ninja stuff. When a customer is telling you something, write it down, take notes if you can. Why is that important? Because whatever a customer tells you, in the order that they tell you, at a psychologically conscious or unconscious level, is significant. The first thing they tell you is the most important thing to them. And then the second most important thing, and then the third most important thing. You got it? Noting the things important to your customer in order can help you help them according to what is most important to them. Later, we're going to teach you some techniques of how to clarify to make sure that you're on the right track. But to start, just write it down, take some notes exactly as they say it if possible, and then read it back to the customer. You want to make sure that the customer is getting exactly what they want or at least that you know exactly what they want. We're going to have to see whether or not you can deliver it depending on your policies and what it is the customer is asking for. But the biggest thing at this time is just knowing what the customer wants and letting them know that you understand exactly what they want.

Repeating what the customer wants brings us to the second part. You have to actively listen to what the customer is saying. Okay? Have you ever been in a conversation with somebody about a topic you love, and it's a great conversation? Maybe you're so excited that you're just thinking of the next thing to say, right? You're like, "Would you just stop talking, so I can tell you my thing?" Does that ever happen? Yeah, so active listening is when you're actually fully engaged, and you're actually more concerned about what the other person has to say than what you want to say next. If you're engaged, you're making eye contact. You're not formulating what your response is going to be. You're just completely taking in the information from the person. That's active listening, and it is a skill that good leaders and great customer service workers develop.

Passive listening is when you're formulating your answer before they're even done speaking. Or you're thinking about, you know, the football game. Or you're thinking about something else that happened while somebody is talking to you. While you might be physically present, if you're listening passively, you're not hearing them. Remember, all of your customers want to be heard. In order to do that, you have to actively listen to what the customer is saying. I hope that makes sense.

Next, number three, acknowledge verbally that you are actively listening. Every now and then use this great phrase, "I understand," or "Yes, of course." Okay? While you're making eye contact, while you're engaged, and while you're present in that conversation.

I had an entertainment company years ago, and we were based out of Beverly Hills, so we did a lot of parties for film studios, we did a lot of corporate events, we did a lot of celebrity events. And I'll never forget this one year when we were blessed enough to actually do an after party for the Academy Awards, for one of the big studios. We had these meetings, and we brought in our teams and one of the things we were providing was a DJ. And they told us, they said, there's this one particular song, it's this disco song, that they just didn't want played. They thought it was cheesy, they thought it was overplayed and overdone. Their only request was that we avoid this song, just one song. Out of the millions of songs out there, they didn't want one particular song. I said, "Great! That's easy. That is super easy." We listened and understood. Well, there was another guy who was in the room with me and he was the DJ.

I'll never forget what happened; I'm downstairs, and the DJ who was in the meeting is DJing from this DJ booth, and there're all these peoples; there're celebrities everywhere, there's paparazzi, everybody is in their tuxes. I mean, this was a great night. And all of a sudden, I hear the first few bars of that particular disco song that the client didn't want. Everything stopped and was in slow motion. I heard radios going off, I heard people just upset; the client came and grabbed me and put their hand on my shoulder and asked me, "What is going on?" You have to actively listen to exactly what your customers want. And how did that end? The party was great, everybody had a great time, but I lost that client. I lost that client and didn't get that client back for years. And years later, I actually did do another event for them, and they still remembered the incident. That's how important actively listening is.

Let's review. You have to listen intently. Listen exactly to what the customer wants, not what you want to hear, and take notes if possible. Next, actively listen to what the customer is saying. Do not get caught up in formulating your response. Acknowledge verbally that you are actively listening with, "I understand. Yes, of course." Okay? And then you have to deliver whatever it is they're looking for. Alright, we'll catch you in the next chapter.

Reflections on YOUR customer service:

What are three things you can do to let your customer know you are actively listening to them?

How does the first thing let them know you hear them?

How does the second thing let them know you hear them?

How does the third thing let them know you hear them?

"One thing talk can't accomplish. . . is
communication. This is because everybody's
talking too much to pay attention to
what anyone else is saying."

–P. J. O'Rourke

CHAPTER 9

CUSTOMER SERVICE: VERBAL AND NONVERBAL CUES

In this chapter, we're going to continue looking at how to understand your customers. This next piece is very important: it is verbal and nonverbal cues. Verbal and nonverbal cues. What does that mean? Verbal cues are things that people might say, even under their breath. If you're trying to, you know, bring them down from being upset, and you're trying to provide a remedy, and you're telling them about the remedy and they're like, "Oh, pfft," or "Oh, great. . ." That's a verbal cue. Right? And so many times we just want to get the customers in and out, or we're restricted with what we can do to serve them that we just gloss over that verbal cue. Some of you don't do that; some of you do.

Verbal cues are an overt expression from a customer. We don't want to gloss over them, and we're going to give you some tools on how to handle them.

What about a nonverbal cue? Maybe you're explaining a remedy to an upset customer, and they're just looking at their watch or frowning. That's a nonverbal cue, right? You have to be able to pick up on that. And the same thing when you're doing a good job. If your remedy is helping, they'll be nodding their head or maybe they'll be smiling. Those are more nonverbal cues. Similarly, some positive verbal cues might be, "Oh, awesome." Or "Oh, that's great. That's exactly what I'm looking for." These things tell you that you're on the right track. Listen and acknowledge the vocal tone, the vocal volume, sighing, and the word choice, so you don't miss anything. Why is this important? Here are the numbers: ninety-six percent of your unhappy customers won't tell you they're unhappy. Ninety-one percent of them simply don't come back. That's big. How is that affecting your client base? Think about all the clients who are upset. Ninety-six percent of your unhappy customers won't even tell you they're unhappy and ninety-one percent of them just won't come back. It is that easy to lose a customer and lose potential profits.

You have to notice and respond to those nonverbal cues—the body language, frowning, shallow breathing, right? You can't just gloss over those things either. You have to address them. And number three, look for the meaning behind the words and respond appropriately.

I'll give you an example. I travel quite a bit, and I'm part of a rewards program for a particular hotel and they have awesome customer service. That's why I'm in the rewards program, because I really enjoy staying at this hotel. But not too long ago I was, gosh, I was in Atlanta; I walked in and the person looked at me, and it was like I was intruding on her parade. This was the person behind the counter! She looked at me and gave me one of those sighs and eye rolls. Her nonverbal cue, right? She didn't even make eye contact or ask for my name. I said, "Yes, I'm David Brownlee, I'm here to check in." And all of a sudden, she starts going through the rigmarole, "Thank you for being a platinum member. (Sigh.) We know you have a lot of choices, and you get a free thing from our market and this is how. . ." She was saying the right words, but her verbal and nonverbal cues, how did those make me feel? Not like a platinum member, I'll tell you that. And then she found out who I was and that I'm an international customer service speaker, and she pepped up a little bit, but boy, that's not such a great way to do it. First, she started the interaction with a negative nonverbal stance, and she avoided any meaningful engagement, which totally betrayed the positive experiences I had had with this hotel. Even when she decided that I was someone special, her attempt to provide superior customer service was totally lost.

Let's review. You have to listen and acknowledge the vocal tone. If you can tell that somebody's still upset, address it. And you can ask them a question. (We're going to talk about this as well.) You can ask them a question like, "Is that an excellent remedy for it?" or "If I could do this for you, would that help you?" Or, "Would that make you feel better?" Or, "Would that make you happy?" Right? You have to address it. And that's a good thing. It might take a little more work on your end. You might have to get a little more creative. It might take a little more time, but it's worth it. I don't believe your customer is always right, but they should always leave happy. And we're going to expand on that because ninety-six percent of your unhappy customers won't tell you they're unhappy, and ninety-one percent of them just won't come back. You have to notice and respond to nonverbal cues—the body language, the frowning, shallow breathing—and look for the meaning behind the words that they're using and respond appropriately. Does that make sense? Alright, you guys have got this. Let's think about verbal and nonverbal cues for a moment, then we'll see you in the next chapter, and we're going to continue on the topic of your responses.

Reflections on YOUR customer service:

What are three verbal or nonverbal positive cues you can look for to make sure that you are communicating with your customers in a positive, meaningful way?

____

____

____

____

____

What is the customer really communicating by the first cue?

____

____

____

____

____

What is the customer really communicating by the second cue?

____

____

____

____

____

What is the customer really communicating by the third cue?

____

____

____

____

____

What are three verbal or nonverbal negative cues you can look for to make sure that you are communicating with your customers in a positive, meaningful way?

How can you respond to the first cue to make the customer feel better?

What is the customer really communicating by the second cue?

What is the customer really communicating by the third cue?

"Failure is not the opposite of
success; it's part of success."

—Arianna Huffington

YOUR RESPONSIBILITY TO YOUR CUSTOMER

In this chapter, we're going to focus on your response and your responsibility to your clients. Your response and your responsibility. What does that mean? If you have an upset customer, or just a customer you're trying to serve by finding a solution for them, your response is crucial. And if somebody had a problem, you need to take responsibility for it. Here's an example. Somebody calls you. They're upset, and they're not really upset at you, they're upset at your coworker, or they're upset with something that your company did. Right? And it wasn't even your fault. How do you react? Do you tell them, "Oh, pfft, those guys down in shipping; they're always screwing up," or "Oh, wow, Jack. Jack's horrible. I can't believe he did that to you." This doesn't solve anything (but it might damage the company reputation). The client on the other side: do they care if it's Jack, or the shipping department, or the company? No. They want a solution. And if you happen to pick up the phone, or you happen to be there standing in front of that person who's upset, you need to take responsibility. You take responsibility to try to help them. Why? Because, in that moment, you represent your company. You represent Jack over there. You represent your shipping department. You're the face that represents your company, good or bad, okay? And your response is going to set the tone for the transaction that happens next.

The first thing you want to do is reassure the customer. Reassure the customer that you are trying to help. Put the customer at ease, so they know you're there to serve them and take care of them. Remember? Your clients want to be taken care of. You might say something like, "I will do whatever I can to make sure we resolve this for you ASAP." That's a great thing to say. Or you might say this to reassure the customer: "I'm here now, and I promise to take excellent care of you." Saying "I'm here now"—what does that do? It says, hey, listen, it doesn't matter who else you've dealt with or what else happens, I'm here, and I promise—oh, people love that word—I promise to take excellent care of you. Now, be aware, you're not promising to give them exactly what they want because you don't know what that is or if you can even do it. But you promise to take excellent care of them. Okay?

And the next thing, you might say something like this, "I will do everything I can to make sure you leave happy." Because the customer is not always right, but they always what? They always leave happy. And tell them that. Say, "I will do everything I can do to make sure you leave happy. Would you like this?" And what else are you doing for yourself? You're giving yourself some time and space. If they are in agreement with that sentence, they've unconsciously just agreed with you, so it won't be as hard for them to do it again. If you say, "We're going to work through this thing," you've got some time now to work through their problem and find a solution that works for them so they leave happy. Once they agree with you that your goal is to make them leave happy, their focus just went from being upset to leaving happy. Does that make sense? The power of your words can direct what they're going to focus on. And whatever they focus on is going to determine how they feel. If they're upset and you're saying, "No, no, no, it's our company policy, blah blah blah. . . ," how is that going to make them feel? You're keeping their focus in the negative. You want to push their focus through your words, through your actions, through your tone, through your caring, to push them in a positive direction, and we're going to look more at this as we turn to positive communication.

I bought this day planner, and I was excited for it, right? It's a day planning company that I've been using for the past few years, and I'm old school. I like to write things down. I do use mobile apps, many devices, and I use the cloud and all that stuff, but I also like to write, especially when I'm on the phone with somebody. I like to write down some information. I'm waiting for this day planner. They send it to me, and I'm excited. I rip open the box, look in, and there it is. It's got my inserts. I put the inserts inside the planner, and I go to close the binder and the little teeth that are supposed to line up don't line up. I'm like, "What?" And when I try to take the sheet of paper to put it in the teeth, those don't line up, either. It is totally useless. The company said, "That's okay, we're going to take care of it. Send it back, and we'll send you out another one." Nothing happens, nothing happens; finally I call them and they tell me, "Oh, it's the manufacturer. The manufacturer sucks and the shipping. . ." They tell me all kinds of stuff. And I'm like okay, great, well where's my planner? They just kept blaming everybody else without sending a planner, and it took, oh gosh, maybe two or three months before I actually got the day planner. What was I doing during that time? I had to come up with some other systems—a lot more cloud and a lot more digital—until I got the planner. But the customer service agents in the company were blaming everybody else; there was no responsibility. And the response? It was certainly not ASAP. You have to ask yourself what can you do to make your service friendlier, to make it faster, and to make it easier for your clients? Returning to my day planner, what was the result of this poor customer service experience? Well, it forced me to adapt to a planning platform that I was previously unfamiliar with, and I never purchased another planner from that company. Although

I had no intention of discontinuing my use of this company's product, they lost me as a returning customer.

To review, let's go back to the idea of response and responsibility. You have to reassure the customer. Put the customer at ease! You know that you're there to serve them and take care of them. Say things like, "I will do whatever I can to make sure that we resolve this for you ASAP." And then you have to do it, right? You can reassure them by saying, "I'm here now, and I promise to take excellent care of you." And third, say things like, "I will do everything I can to make sure you leave happy." This turns the customer's focus away from the problem (negative) and to the solution (positive). Got it? Awesome. Let's think about this for a moment, and I'll see you guys in the next chapter.

Reflections on YOUR customer service:

Why is it important for you to take responsibility for your coworker's mistakes if you are the one talking with the customer in that moment?

____

____

____

____

____

____

____

____

____

____

What is the result of you taking the responsibility of another person's mistake in your company?

____

____

____

____

____

____

____

____

____

____

"The price of inaction is far greater
than the cost of a mistake."

—MEG WHITMAN

CHAPTER 11

RESPONDING QUICKLY TO YOUR CUSTOMERS

In this chapter, we're going to continue to look at response and responsibility in customer service. For good customer service, you have to respond quickly. You have to show the customer that their request is important and take action right away. Whether that's sending an email, making a phone call, or just beginning to work on a solution, speed is important. Why? Well, for starters, seventy-eight percent of consumers have bailed on a transaction or not made the intended purchase because of poor customer service. I'll say that again: seventy-eight percent of consumers have bailed on a transaction or not made the intended purchase because of poor customer service. Has that ever happened to you? Where the customer service was so bad, you're like, you know what, I don't even want your product or service anymore? I'm out of here. I'm going to go find somebody else. To avoid losing this type of customer, you have to show the customer that their request is important and take action right away. Especially if they're upset, but even if they're not upset.

Years ago, I was in Paris. I was there with my wife and some friends of ours, and we were doing some shopping. We were in this great area, and I think I even bought a scarf. An American buying a scarf, go figure. We're walking around and we're looking for different things, and I notice my buddy has on a pretty cool backpack. And I needed a backpack at the time. I'm like dude, that's a pretty cool backpack. He told me a little bit about it, and I took a look at it. Didn't think much more of it. We get back to the States, and I'm in San Diego and I get an email from my buddy. It says, "Hey, this website has that same backpack on sale for fifty percent off." I go, "Oh, that's pretty cool." This is about five o'clock at night. I went online, I purchased it, and I figured I'd get it in a few days. I put it on my credit card and sent the order off. The next morning, about nine o'clock, I get a knock on my door, and it's a delivery guy. I'm like, "Whoa, what does this guy have? I don't remember ordering anything?" I sign for the package, and guess what it is? It's the backpack that I ordered sixteen hours before! Whoa, that was quick. That was really quick. It totally blew me away. I was like, this place is amazing! And it was the exact backpack that I wanted; everything was great. Okay? See how that company went beyond my expectation. I'm still talking about that experience, and really the only thing they did differently was take care of their customer with speed.

Show the customer that their request is important and take action right away. We live in what I like to call "the microwave society." We want it now; we want it right now! And sometimes I hear from clients, "Oh, our customers are just too demanding." Well, it's not that they're too demanding, it's that other companies are serving them faster, friendlier, making it more fantastic. And we need to constantly be thinking about how we can do that for our customers as well. You might say that to them: "I will take care of this for you right away." That feels good. This person is going to take care of this for me right away? Awesome. Or, you can say, "We will have this resolved for you ASAP." Now, you're not giving them a time zone. You're not saying okay, in the next ten minutes. Maybe you can take ten minutes, ten hours, ten days, ten weeks; it doesn't matter. ASAP means "as soon as possible." Whatever that looks like with your system, or whatever the problem is, you're going to take care of it, ASAP. By letting them know that you're handling their product or issue ASAP, you're reassuring them, aren't you?

To review, you want to respond to customers quickly. Show the customer that their request is important and take action right away. Send that email, make a phone call, and begin working on a solution. Don't just dilly-dally around. Why? Because seventy-eight percent of consumers have bailed on a transaction, or not made an intended purchase, because of poor customer service. What types of things can you say to people? "I will take care of this for you right away," or "We will have this resolved for you ASAP."

Alright, good work. Let's think about this, and I'm going to see you guys in the next chapter.

Reflections on YOUR customer service:

What are three ways (using words or actions) you can demonstrate to your customers that you are responding quickly to their requests?

____

____

____

____

How does the first way let the customer know you're taking care of them?

____

____

____

____

How does the second way let the customer know you're taking care of them?

____

____

____

____

How does the third way let the customer know you're taking care of them?

____

____

____

____

"Customers don't care about your policies.
Find and engage the need.
Tell the customer what you can do."

—ALICE SESAY POPE

CHAPTER 12

IMPLEMENTING POSITIVE COMMUNICATION

In this chapter, we're going to continue looking at the very important topic of response and responsibility. Now, I love this section because here's what we're going to discuss: positive communication. When a customer makes a request, or challenges you, you want to respond positively. Respond positively. What does that mean? You know, since we were little kids, we were doing things we shouldn't do and our parents told us, "No, no! I said no!" Can I have this thing? "No!" Can I do . . .? "No!" How does that feel after a while? Right? For kids it might get old, but they don't have a choice, but our customers do. Negative communication is a great way to get a customer to begin thinking of going somewhere else for their product or service. Especially when transactions are involved; when we're spending money. Can I do this? "No!" Can I get a little extra . . .? "No!" How can we just say yes to our customers instead? How can we say yes? Or at least, how can we avoid the word no? If there's something we just can't deliver, how can we avoid responding with "No?"

Are you guys up for a challenge? This is fun. We do this in companies all over the country. And what we do is we challenge the customer service reps, and we challenge the staff, to avoid using the word "no." You have to get a little creative, and I'm going to give you some tips on how to do it. Want to know what those are? Great, here we go.

Do everything you can to avoid the word no. What can you say instead? This is one of my favorites: "Ah, I wish I could, but what I can do for you is . . ." I like that. "I wish I could. What I can do for you is . . ." I'll give you an example from my own business. There was a company that wanted to hire me to come do a speaking engagement. And that's great. I love doing them; I've been in special events for, gosh, twenty plus years now. I've been a speaker for a long time, so I understand the industry. And one thing that I learned is that after the event is over, there's not a whole lot of encouragement or not a whole lot of leverage to get paid on time, right? The event's over, I've done my piece, but I haven't been paid. Long ago we switched our policies. We're still giving excellent customer service, but we changed our policies so in order for the client to reserve a speaking date, a fifty percent deposit is required and then the balance needs to be paid before the event. Pretty simple. Most clients understand this. They get it. But this particular client was used to paying net forty-five. And what that means is that after the event, they'll pay me forty-five days later . . . maybe. But that's what net forty-five means. And typically, big companies, that's what they do, right? It helps their cash flow, so they do net forty-five. But for us, we're a small business; it doesn't work for us.

I get this email and the company is asking for net forty-five payment terms, and I said, "Well, I wish I could. What I can do for you is . . ." Because I knew that they wanted to stretch their money, what I told them is that they can do the deposit and what I can do for them is instead of sending the balance of the check seven days before the speaking engagement, they can have a check ready right there. Once I arrive, then they can pay me the rest. Okay? "What I can do for you is . . ." And they were fine with that! That was great! And it worked out for them and so, there you go. I didn't say, "No, that's our policy, you're going to rip me off, and you're not going to pay me and . . ." No, instead, I avoided no by saying, "Hey, I wish I could. What I can do for you is . . ." And that compromise worked and everybody was happy. Okay? And I knew a lot of information on the front end by asking intelligent questions to make sure I was correct in my assessment of why they wanted net forty-five, so I was able to find a mutually beneficial compromise. Okay? It is possible to avoid saying no while still allowing everything to come together, and you can connect the dots.

Next, take responsibility for the customer's issue, regardless of whose fault it is. Okay? We talked about that before. It doesn't matter if it's the shipping department's fault or if it's accounting's fault, or if it's Jack's fault. Or maybe your customer is having billing problems. Oh, those are huge! Anybody ever go through some billing issues? Those customers are upset, aren't they? Because it has to do with their money. Take responsibility, even if you work in customer service and the problem is with billing. Okay? Take responsibility for the customer's issue, regardless of whose fault it is.

Here's another little ninja trick. Do you guys want a ninja phrase? You do? Okay, here's the ninja phrase. Instead of saying, "I'm sorry," say something else. Right, when you tell somebody, "I'm sorry," it dies with "I'm sorry." You're just saying, "Hey, look, I'm sorry," but it doesn't change anything. What's better is, "I apologize," or "please forgive me." I love "please forgive me," because now you're asking somebody to *do* something and now, they're engaged with you. It's just a little two-millimeter shift in the language we use and the communication that we use to move us towards a positive outcome. This is all part of the game; avoid saying, "no" and avoid saying, "I'm sorry." Instead use, "I apologize" or "Please forgive me." Okay? This is all part of responding positively. Responding positively is a wonderful way to keep control of the tone of conversations with customers. Do everything you can to avoid the word "no." Use instead, "I wish I could. What I can do for you is . . ." Take responsibility for the customer's issue, regardless of whose fault it is, and use "I apologize" or "Please forgive me." Alright? Awesome. I'm going to see you guys in the next chapter.

Reflections on YOUR customer service:

Imagine three recent customer requests that you could not accommodate. How could you have used the phrase, "I wish I could. What I can do for you is (fill in the blank)." to respond to the customer?

____

____

____

____

____

____

What are two alternative ways to say "I'm sorry"?

____

____

____

____

____

____

Why specifically is saying "Will you forgive me?" more effective than saying "I'm sorry?"

____

____

____

____

____

____

"How you think about your customer
influences how you respond to them."

—MARILYN SUTTLE

CHAPTER 13

YOUR MOST POWERFUL TOOL IN CUSTOMER SERVICE

In this chapter, we're going to talk about how to use empathy in customer service. What is empathy? Empathy is really putting yourself in the customer's shoes. And, gosh, years ago, I had an issue with my phone company. What ended up happening was that I had this crazy bill to Australia while I was giving a seminar. Supposedly, I was on the phone to Australia. And the only Australians I know live here in the States! It wasn't me. There was a mistake, something happened. Something went wrong. So clearly, it's going to be easy to get through it, right? Oh, no, no, no. I called the company and as soon as I called this company, there was something up. They were ready to go to battle. They're looking at my account, they're doing whatever, and this guy almost sounded like a robot. He was like, "No. No. There's nothing we can do. No." And it was a conversation that wasn't going anywhere, so I decided to change it up. I wanted to step out of where we were and step into just having a civil, human conversation. I asked him, "Hey, can we just be human for a second? Let's just be human." And I asked him straight up, "Has anything like this ever happened to you before?" His response was, "Yes." And I said, "Okay, good, so how did that make you feel?" He responded, "Bad." I came back with, "Okay, so what did you end up doing?" "I paid it," he responded with an uncomfortable laugh. What? There was no empathy in this guy at all! I hang up the phone, and I'm getting ready to call back and hopefully get a different customer service rep, right? I'm like I want somebody else.

But one thing I do get, even before I can call back—and this is funny—I get a customer service text: "How would you rate that call?" I'm like zero, zero, zero, right? I'm fuming! And what happens? Lo and behold, my phone rings. I get a phone call from the phone company. Oh, this is going to be great. Now I've got somebody elevated from robot-man who is really going to make me feel good and take care of my problem. Oh, wouldn't that have been nice? Instead, I get somebody else, some elevated person, who just came to the phone with a helmet on and with a shield and a sword, just ready to fight. It was worse than talking to robot guy! I hang up. I had a speaking engagement, and I had to leave for Arizona. I'm like, when I get back, I'm switching companies.

The next day, I'm in Arizona, and I'm going to dinner and my phone rings. Eight hundred number, I pick it up, and it's a guy from this company. I said, "Wow, man, I'm switching. I'm out of here, I'm gone. As soon as I get back to San Diego, I'm out of here, and I'm switching companies." He goes, "Oh, listen, I understand. I would feel the same way. I can only imagine how that would be frustrating." And I look at the phone and said, "What?" This guy's absolutely amazing. I respond to him, "Hey look, I'm going to dinner right now. Could I just hang up and call you back?" He says, "Oh, gosh, I wish I could, but if you call back, you might get somebody else." I say, "That's it, buddy, you're coming to dinner with me." I took the phone with me, and we talked through it over dinner. He resolved it, and got me my refund. Now, how cool was that? And they could, by the way, have done the exact same thing on the first phone call. They could have done the same thing on the second phone call. All while keeping me a little bit mellower. So, the company solved my problem and kept my business, but still left a bad taste in my mouth. With a bit of empathy from either of the first two customer service representatives, I might have become a bigger fan of the company. Instead, because of their very non-empathetic tone, I remained with them, but not as an enthusiastic customer.

To review this chapter, what is empathy in customer service? It is putting yourself in the customer's shoes. Okay? Think about a time, maybe, when you were in a similar situation. What do you say to let the customer know that you're putting yourself in their shoes? You say, "I understand." Again, your customers want to be understood. Okay? Number two, you can say, "I would feel the same way!" Wouldn't you? If you were actually being empathetic, and you were listening intently, would you feel the same way? Would you be upset if x, y, or z happened? Okay? If you would feel the same way, tell them, "You know what? I would feel the same way." And number three, you can say, "I can imagine how that would be frustrating." I can imagine how that would be frustrating. Super simple. And just by you doing that, your customer will feel heard, and they'll feel understood. Now you just need to provide that remedy so that they feel cared for. And this is sending you down that track to them feeling cared for, isn't it? Put yourself in the customer's shoes; that's empathy. "I understand." "I would feel the same way." "I can imagine that would be frustrating." In the next chapter, we're going to talk about some more ways you can really show empathy in your customer service to better overcome your customer's challenges. We'll see you in the next chapter.

Reflections on YOUR customer service:

What are three things you can say to a customer to help them know that you care and understand how they feel?

____

____

____

____

____

____

How does the first thing let the customer know you want to help them?

____

____

____

____

How does the second thing let the customer know you want to help them?

____

____

____

____

How does the third thing let the customer know you want to help them?

____

____

____

____

"Our attitude towards others determines
their attitude towards us."

—EARL NIGHTINGALE

CHAPTER 14

EMPATHY IN CUSTOMER SERVICE

In this chapter, we're going to continue to look at how to use empathy in customer service, so you can better overcome your customer's challenges. Really think if you're listening to somebody intently, or think about or recall a similar situation that you have been in. Okay?

I'll give you an example. Your customer is explaining a problem to you or a challenge that they've had and, lo and behold, you've had a similar challenge. You might say something to them like, "Something similar happened to me when x, y, and z." Wow. You've just clearly shown that you can identify exactly with what the customer is experiencing.

By stating your similar situation to the customer, now you're building rapport with them, you're relating to them. "Something similar happened to me when . . . ," and you tell your part of the story. Now how does that make the customer feel? It makes them realize that they're not alone, not crazy. They're thinking, "I'm just going through this problem! And you know what? The person who is helping me has been through this problem as well." What's great is, once you have that relationship and that bond, now they'll be looking to you like, "Okay, so how did you get out of this?" You might say something like,

"When I went through this, I found that the best remedy was this," or "I found that to overcome this was to do this," or "I found that this is how the system works, and this is what I have to do differently." Okay? Now the customer is starting to come to you and build that rapport and look to you for the answers. And hopefully you'll have the answer, or at least be able to get to somebody who does have the answer.

To review, let the customer know you can relate to them. You might say, "Well, I can relate because this happened to me." Right? Now you're relating, you're recalling a similar situation, and that's called empathy. Right? "Something similar happened to me when x, y, z." or "When I went through this, I found that . . ." And I love that sentence too, by the way. If you have somebody who might be wrong about something, rather than saying, "You know what, you're totally wrong, that's crap. This is how it really goes," you can say, "Well, when I went through this, I found that . . ." and tell them the truth. Tell them what the reality is, right? That way they're not losing face or anything, you're just explaining your story, your situation. And again, they're looking to you for the answer—to solve their issue. Next, you might say, "I can relate because x, y, z was a similar situation to what you went through." Easy stuff? But so powerful! So powerful. Okay? That's it for this chapter, I'll see you guys in the next one.

Reflections on YOUR customer service:

What are three reasons why empathy is important to your customer service?

"People don't care how much you know
until they know how much you care."

—THEODORE ROOSEVELT

CHAPTER 15

SHOWING GENUINE CONCERN FOR YOUR CUSTOMERS

In this chapter, we're going to continue looking at empathy in customer service, okay? The next thing you want to do is you really, truly want to show concern for your client or your customer. You want to actually show them concern. What does that mean? That means that if somebody's telling you something, you're actively listening, and you're asking intelligent questions. Show some actual concern! If somebody's telling you a problem, and you're just sitting there grinning and doing nothing, you might get slapped. Okay? Or at least the customer will feel like slapping you, because you're not showing concern. Or, if somebody's telling you something, and you're using verbal or nonverbal cues like, oh, here we go again . . . That's not showing concern. People want to be taken care of. You might tell them, "I will make sure that you are taken care of," or "I will make sure we get you the replacement right away." Okay? Or, "I will make sure you are happy, excited, and more than satisfied with our solution." Or, "I will make sure you are happy with our solution." Okay? Whatever the solution is. It might be exactly what they're talking about in the beginning. It might be something completely different. But whatever that is, you are going to do everything you can to make sure that client is taken care of. Does that make sense? Okay, excellent.

Showing concern—that's empathy. That's going to be huge in helping you get those upset customers down to earth with you. "I will make sure that you're taken care of. I will make sure that we'll get you x. I'll make sure that you're happy with our solution." And when you put all this together, and you actually do truly care about your client, this stuff comes easily, doesn't it? Think about if you have kids or somebody you love—a family member, a friend, a husband, or a wife. Do you naturally show empathy for them? Like when they get hurt—when your kid gets hurt, you want to put them in your lap and make them feel better and give them a Band-Aid, right? Or when your spouse is hurt or has been through a rough day or something, don't you want to give them a hug and show empathy for them? Show them that you care. That's what this is about. Show your customers that you care. Treat them like you never want them to leave. Treat them the same way you'd treat anyone else—with empathy. Okay? Show concern. "I'll make sure that you're taken care of. I will make sure that we get you x. I will make sure that you are happy with our solution." Alright, you are all rock stars! Let's think about this for a minute, and I will see you guys in the next chapter.

Reflections on YOUR customer service:

What are three ways you can show genuine concern for your customers when they have an issue with your product or service?

____

____

____

____

____

____

How does the first way let the customer know you want to help them?

____

____

____

____

How does the second way let the customer know you want to help them?

____

____

____

____

How does the third way let the customer know you want to help them?

____

____

____

____

"Customer experiences that eliminate confusion, uncertainty and anxiety reap the rewards, generating a competitive advantage, loyalty and a peerless brand image."

—MATT WATKINSON

CHAPTER 16

CLARIFICATION WITH YOUR CUSTOMERS

Clarify, clarify, clarify! That's what we're going to discuss in this chapter: the importance of clarification with your customers. Have you ever had this problem where a client comes in, and they tell you whatever they tell you, and you're like, "Okay, we're going to get to work on this right away." And you start working to solve the problem. You come up with this great solution, you give it to the customer, and what do they tell you? "Oh, well, that's not my actual problem . . . I wanted this." Has that ever happened to you? Clarification. That's what we need. It's going to help your orders be more accurate. It's going to help you recommend the best service. It's going to really help your clients feel cared for, understood, and heard. Okay? What do you do? The easiest way to clarify is to repeat the request. Right from the beginning, whatever it is that they're requesting. What I do is I write down notes as I ask intelligent questions to my clients. I do this in order to find out exactly what they're looking for. And then, I'll read it back to them. "So, if I'm hearing you correctly, you're looking for a, b, and c." Now, nine times out of ten they'll say, "Yes, that's exactly what I'm looking for." Even if you write it down exactly word for word, sometimes they'll say, "Oh, well, that's not exactly what I meant. What I really want is x, y, and z." You clarify again, right? You repeat the customer's second request word for word to show that you are listening and that you want to get them exactly what they are looking for. That's going to help them feel heard and understood as well.

Clarification will also help avoid confusion when you try to solve the problem and will ensure you're working to solve the customer's actual problem. Make sure you know exactly what the requests are, exactly what the problem is, and that your solution is going to solve the customer's actual problem. You have to clarify. You know who is great at this? Fast food restaurants. Because things are moving; things are moving quickly so fast food counter staff are instructed to repeat your order. If you put in an order, they repeat that order for you exactly. Nowadays, they've got those screens, right? Here you can get this big burger, this heart attack in a box, and this giant drink of liquid sugar or whatever it is, and after you order, the cashier will repeat it and say, "Is that the accurate order?" And they'll clarify with you, right? And then you can still get the order wrong, but okay, you see where I'm going with this, right? You want to do whatever you can to clarify.

To clarify further, you might say something like, "So, to confirm, you're looking for x, y, z. What I'm hearing you say is you would like a, b, c." Now you're making sure that you're on the same page as the client and that you are engaged with each other. Now your starting place gives you a foundation for whatever comes next, right? For whatever is next in that remedy. Whatever is next in providing your service, right? The best service, or the best product for them, because that's what is going to be important. But you have to clarify.

Does that make sense? Okay, good. You got this. Repeat the request. Repeat the customer's request word for word to show that you're listening. Number two: clarification will avoid confusion when you try to solve your customer's problem (or complete their order).

And it will ensure you're working on the right problem—that your solution actually solves the customer's problem. You might say things like, "so, to confirm," or "What I'm hearing you say is you'd like x, y, z." Okay? Excellent. Alright, I'm going to see you guys in the next chapter.

Reflections on YOUR customer service:

What are three reasons why clarification is important in your customer service?

"If you are going to move mountains
for your customers, make sure
you're moving the right one."

—DAVID BROWNLEE

CHAPTER 17

RULE #1: CLARIFY.
RULE #2: SEE RULE #1.

In this chapter, we're going to continue to talk about clarification—clarify, clarify, clarify. In order to clarify, you need to confirm your customer's desired outcome. In the last chapter, we highlighted confirming your customer's request, right? What do they want at the beginning? Now, what do they want at the end? The conversation transforms from understanding the request to understanding the final outcome. Okay? We have to clarify what they're looking for as an outcome. You might say, "What I'm hearing you say is that you ultimately want x." Why is this important? Because sometimes a client will get so focused in on one little aspect of their challenge, whatever it is with your product or your service, one little aspect of a larger picture, and they just hone in on that. And that may or may not be something you can overcome. Now, if you can get them to focus on what they ultimately want, a lot of times you can go right around that thing they want fixed or changed. Sometimes, that little thing becomes insignificant if there is a solution that ultimately solves the larger issue. Does that make sense?

You want to clarify what they're ultimately trying to get. If your client goes back to this little thing that may or may not be important (many times, it's not), you can refocus them onto what they ultimately want. Okay? In order to do that, you need to ask intelligent questions to find out what they ultimately want, and you have to clarify. You might say something like this: "If I can do x—the customer's desired outcome—for you, would that be an excellent solution for you?" Or, "If I can get you a full refund, would that be an excellent solution for you?" Or, "If I can change those dates for you, would that be an excellent solution for you?" That's clarifying! They're either going to say yes or no. And if they say no, that's okay. Don't just gloss over it and say, "Oh, well, there's nothing else I can do, blah blah blah." It's going to take a little more work, right? You may have to talk to a manager, you may have to go back to a manager, you might have to start thinking outside the box. You may have to refocus them on their desired outcome. Okay?

If a client is not excited about your solution, you may say something like, "What would be an outstanding solution for this issue?" Again, a scary word because now you're asking them what they actually want. But when I ask you what you want, how does that make you feel? Cared for, right? I care! I'm showing empathy! "What would be an outstanding solution for this issue?" Now I'm putting the ball in your court. And again, you could say something totally outlandish and there's no way I could get it for you, and I might use my old trick of avoiding no by saying, "Well, I wish I could, but what I can do for you is x, y, z." If it's really outlandish, you know, depending on your rapport, you can have some fun with them: "Oh, gosh, ha ha, that would be great." Right? If your client is not excited about your solution, you really want to make sure you ask them, "What would be an outstanding solution for this issue?" See what feedback you get. Nine times out of ten, it's going to be reasonable. Even if it's reasonable, you may or may not be able to accommodate it. You're showing empathy. You're showing that they've been heard. You're showing that you care for them. You're showing that you understand them. And, a lot of times, even if a client can't get their desired outcome, because you showed that effort, they'll still continue to be a client. And they'll still really think that you're giving them excellent customer service. Does that make sense?

To recap: confirm your customer's desired outcome. Use questions such as, "What I'm hearing you say is that you ultimately want x," or "If I can do (customer's desired outcome), will that be an excellent solution for you?" Get the response and respond accordingly. If a client is not excited about your solution, find out what an outstanding solution for this issue would be. You got it. Alright guys, I'm going to see you in the next chapter.

Reflections on YOUR customer service:

What are three reasons why it is important to clarify the solutions that you offer to your customers?

"We must learn what customers really want, not what they say they want or what we think they should want."

—ERIC RIES

CHAPTER 18

CLARIFYING THE SOLUTION WITH YOUR CUSTOMERS

In this chapter, we're going to continue on clarification—clarify, clarify, clarify! I cannot stress that enough! Next, you want to repeat the solution. Now we know exactly what the request is, and we know the exact outcome they're after. Now we want to make sure that your solution is going to ensure that the customer leaves happy. Your customers are not always right, but they always leave happy. We're going to repeat the solution and all of its details to the customer. You can say, "So, here's what we are able to do for you: it's x, y, z." Okay? And you spell it out. You spell it out for them, so that there's no question about what it is that you're going to do for the client or customer. You don't want to gloss over anything.

You also want to check in with the customer. See their reaction to the solution, right? Now you're going to be really looking for those verbal or nonverbal cues. You're listening for those verbal cues, and you're looking for those nonverbal cues. Remember the verbal and nonverbal cues we talked about earlier? What are verbal and nonverbal cues? They are sighing or vocalizations like, "ugh, I just can't believe it." They show you that the customer is upset. Or nonverbal cues include tightly crossed arms or frowning, right? You have to pick up on that. You want to check in with the customer to see their reaction. You want to clarify by paying attention to both the customer's words and body language. You want to make sure that what you're doing is going to make them happy. Simple, right? Good.

You might say something like, "So, to confirm, we will be providing this solution." Then ask them, "Does this work for you?" Or, "How do you feel about that?" And then you pay attention. Listen to the words they tell you. Watch them process that information. Look at how they're responding to it—is their breathing shallow, are they upset, are they talking to somebody else? Or are you moving in the right direction—are they nodding their head like, "Yeah, that sounds fair." Maybe it's even, "Oh my gosh, this is awesome, this is better than what I would have come up with!" Okay? You want to know. You want to clarify, and you clarify by repeating the solution. Repeat the solution and all of its details to the customer. Check in with the customer to see their reaction to the solution, right? As you're looking out for verbal and nonverbal cues, you might say, "So to confirm, we will be providing this solution," or "Does that work for you?" or "How do you feel about that?" Okay? Make sense? Good. You guys got this! I'm going to see you in the next chapter.

Reflections on YOUR customer service:

What are three negative outcomes that might occur if you DON'T clarify the solution to your customer before providing your solution?

Could this have been avoided with clarification?

Could this have been avoided with clarification?

Could this have been avoided with clarification?

"Ask your customers to be part
of the solution, and don't view them
as part of the problem."

—A LAN W EISS

WHAT YOUR CUSTOMERS REALLY WANT FROM YOU

In this chapter, we're going to focus on solutions. Your customers want solutions from your customer service. They want service, right? What are the solutions? The first thing we have to really look at is: what are you going to deliver to your clients or customers? And I don't just mean shipping and delivering. I mean delivering the service, or delivering the product, or delivering the attitude, or delivering the experience. Whatever it is you have to deliver. That's the first part of the solution. For example, if somebody comes to your business, the idea of doing business is they've got a problem, some sort of problem. It could be as simple as needing a stick of gum. Or it could be someone is going through some sort of legal challenge, and they need a lawyer. It is something; their TV just blew up, and they need a TV. There's some sort of challenge, there's some sort of problem, and challenges require what? Solutions. That's why they come to your business. That's why you're in business. So, big or small, your company exists to provide solutions to problems. You have to first deliver the best suited product or service for the customer that will meet their needs. Again, your goal should be to deliver the best suited product or service for the customer that will meet their needs. Okay?

Similarly, you have to deliver the best quality product or service that will exceed their expectations. Whatever it is they're expecting, what is something extra you could put on there so that you exceed their expectations? That's where the magic happens. Your customer can go to any store to get whatever product or to get whatever service, so you need to exceed expectations. What extra thing can you do to exceed expectations?

Your customers also want one hundred percent accuracy in their order request. Right? If you've clarified everything, hopefully the accuracy will be great. You never know with things like shipping departments and billing and stuff like that, but that's what you're going for. And all of these departments, by the way, are part of your customer service. Okay? If they mess up, it is still your reputation on the line, and as we mentioned earlier, you need to be accountable for any problems from order to receipt of product or service. That's what this section is about. It's not just the interaction that the outward facing employee is having with the customer, right? It's a conversation that includes all people who touch the transaction. Most of what we've talked about in customer service is a two-way conversation, but delivering a product or service is much more than this, and the whole transaction has to be of high quality from start to finish. It has to be accurate, and it has to be suited to really overcoming whatever challenge that the customer might have. Does that make sense?

I'll give you an example. Again, I travel a lot. I take a lot of taxi cabs. And over the years, I've watched the taxi industry customer service go down, down, down. The problem as I witnessed it was at the driver level, the customer-facing level. It got so bad that a cab would pull up, and the cab driver would just sit there. Really, they'd just sit. I've even sometimes had to ask the driver to pop the trunk, so I could put my own luggage in the back of the taxi. Okay? There was a day when taxi cab drivers used to come out, and they'd greet you. They might even have a newspaper for you, and they'd open up the trunk, and they'd put your luggage in. But after time, it went down, down, down.

What happened when taxi cab customer service began to deteriorate? Well, this little company decided, okay, what is everything that is wrong with taxi cabs? Poor customer service—they don't put your bags in, and they sit in traffic so they can watch the meter run and squeeze a couple extra bucks out of you. This ride sharing company—and we know this now, ride sharing—they said, you know what, we're going to put this thing on a mapping system so that you pay an accurate fare. In fact, you're going to know what it is before you ride. And as far as the customer service goes? We're going to let the customers rate drivers on a star system, right? We've talked about review websites, but these review apps within these ride sharing apps are amazing. That really helps your customer service, doesn't it? And they'll have bottles of water for you, they (typically) will get out and grab my bags and put them in the car, they'll give me some friendly conversation, and if they're local to the area, they will tell me what's going on in the area. That is service. That's good service. It's a suited product that solves a problem, right? Because I need a ride. It's a quality product. Sometimes it's a really nice car, and the service is great, and it's accurate. I know what I'm going to pay, they know exactly how to get there, and I know the route they're going to take to get there. It's fantastic. That is delivering a solution. Ask yourself: how can you deliver solutions to your customers in the best way, to make it more fantastic, to make it friendlier, to make it faster? These are the questions we constantly need to be asking ourselves. Because, by the way, once we figure something out, and we're doing pretty good, do we just stay there? No. Customer expectations are always changing and shifting. Whatever we come up with for our customer service system, we need to constantly be thinking and innovating, right? And coming up with that next piece is always important. Does that make sense? Awesome.

To sum up, when it comes to solutions for a customer, you have to deliver. What do you have to deliver? The best suited product or service for the customer that will meet their needs and solve their problem. You have to deliver the best quality product or service that will exceed their expectations. And number three: a hundred percent accuracy in customer orders or requests. Okay? Great job today. I will see you guys in the next chapter.

Reflections on YOUR customer service:

What are three reasons why it is important for you to make sure you are providing the best solution for your customer?

"The more you engage with customers, the clearer things become and the easier it is to determine what you should be doing."

—John Russell

CHAPTER 20

FOLLOWING UP WITH YOUR CUSTOMERS

In this chapter, we are continuing to look at solutions. Your job, as a customer service representative or team member, is to provide solutions for your clients. The next thing you need to do, to really make sure that your solutions are the best they can be, is to follow up. Follow up is big! If you're in retail, you can follow up at the location. How do you do that? Well, you can do it verbally, you can use a comment card, you can give them a complimentary product or service, or you can give them an upgrade. You can ask them something like, for example, "Is there anything else I can do to make this an even better customer service experience for you?" Again, this could be a scary question depending on the business you work for, right? But why is it important to know that while they're at the location? Because while they are at the location, you can do something about it. Because, remember, ninety-six percent of your unhappy customers aren't even going to tell you that they're unhappy, and ninety-one percent of them just won't come back. You want to make sure you ask them, "Is there anything I can do, or could have done, to make this an even better customer experience for you?" Okay? You want to do that at the location whenever possible.

The second way to follow up is on the phone. You can send them a survey, you can give them a free gift, or you can give them a customer care call. These are a few of my favorite ways to follow up. Here is an example of good follow up. I rented from a big rental car company, and this company is amazing with customer service and that's why I use them. I remember, I rented a car, a pretty typical rental, and after my rental, I returned the car, and I gave the rental agent the keys. That night, I got a phone call and somebody said, "Yes, is this Mr. Brownlee?" And I said, "Yeah, this is Mr. Brownlee." They responded, "Oh, this is such and such Rental Car Company . . ." And my first thought was, Hey! It wasn't me! That scratch was already there! I'm a great driver, and it has nothing to do with me! And then all he said was, "We just wanted to make sure that your rental went well. How would you rate the service?" I was like, "Wow, it was great. Everything was great with the rental." I was ecstatic! How would you feel if you made a purchase, or got some sort of service, and they just called you that night to make sure everything was great? That's a customer care call. That's showing your client that they're special. That's giving them significance and letting them know that they're being cared for. And on the phone, you might even ask them, "Is there anything else I can do for you?" Right? Sometimes they may have forgotten to do something or, you know, there's something else, but just offering that is showing the effort and that goes such a long way in that relationship. The funny part about it is, after my rental experience, I would have rated this company a nine or ten. After that call, I think of that company as an eleven, and whenever the topic of car rentals comes up in conversation, guess which company I tell people about?

Email, or even regular mail, is another great way to follow up. You can, again, send a survey or even a thank you card with a coupon or something, if you want them to take action on something. What do we get in the mail nowadays? We get bills. We get, gosh, junk mail. It's a very unused space. There used to be a lot of marketing there, but now it's mostly email. Mail is a great way to follow up with your customers if you want something to be extra special.

Remember when you were a kid, and it would be your birthday or something, or maybe a holiday, and your grandparents or your aunt or your uncle or your good friend, they'd send you what? They'd send you a card in the mail! And you'd open up the card, and if it's your birthday maybe there would be some money in there, and you're like, "Wow!" Right? You'd get that feeling. Same thing can happen with your clients. What if you wrote them a personal thank you card just for being a client, and gave them a coupon or discount? How would they feel? Gestures like this go a long way, and while the coupon or discount might be a bonus, it is the gesture itself that makes your customer know you care. Try it. It's a great way to follow up with your customers and to continue to build that customer relationship, so you get customer loyalty, and they never want to leave you. Again, it is a lot cheaper to keep an existing customer than it is to gain a new one.

Another thing you might do is ask your customer, on a scale from one to ten, how did you do? Even if they give you a nine, you would ask them, "What would have made it a ten for you?" Now you're getting that extra excellence there. And that's where the magic happens. Okay? Take that feedback and—here's the key—when you get the feedback, do something about it! When you get the feedback, you have to make it right. You want to follow up. You can follow up at the location, verbally, or with a comment card or complimentary product or service upgrade. And you might say, "Is there anything else I could have done to make this an even better customer service experience for you?" On the phone, send them a survey, free gift, or make a customer care call, you know: "Is there anything else I can do for you?"

To review, follow up is a critical piece of excellent customer service. Email or mail—send them a survey, send them a thank you card with a coupon and ask them on a scale from one to ten, how did you do? What would have made it a ten? And with the surveys, by the way, I hate those big, long surveys, don't you? Like oh, nice, I had some great service and then you click to do a survey and it's going to take you twenty minutes. Just one question to three questions is about right. My favorite question is, "If you had a customer service training company, would you have hired this person to work for you?" One question, yes or no. Right? Or the question, "On a scale from one to ten, how did we do? What would have made it a ten?" Boom. Super simple for them to share their thoughts with you. Okay? I'm going to see you guys in the next chapter.

Reflections on YOUR customer service:

What are three ways you can follow up with your customers?

What is a possible positive outcome that could result from the first way you follow up?

What is a possible positive outcome that could result from the second way you follow up?

What is a possible positive outcome that could result from the third way you follow up?

"The magic 'mind reading' anticipatory service phrase is: 'If that was me, what would I want?'"

—STEVE COKKINIAS

CHAPTER 21

ANTICIPATING WHAT YOUR CUSTOMERS WANT

In this chapter, we're going to continue talking about solutions. Because that's why you're a customer service representative—to provide solutions for your customers and clients. The next piece is to anticipate future customer needs. This is what helps elevate you those two millimeters. That very small distance that makes a big difference.

The first thing you can do is use their profile and buying history. Okay? You can even do this on the current transaction. How many of you have ever bought something online? Yeah, me too. And I've got little kids, so I'm constantly buying toys, right? I'll go online, and I'll put in my information, and I'll buy the toy. And then it'll say, "People who bought this also bought . . ." And there might be a complimentary toy. Or, my favorite, is batteries. Do you need batteries for this thing? Yeah, because I'm going to order this thing, and it's going to get to my house, and it's not going to have any batteries, and my kids won't be able to play with it. It's awesome. It's like, "Oh, I'm so glad you guys thought of the batteries." Your clients are going to love something like that. It is an up sale for you, and it is beneficial to your customer.

It is important to use your customer's profile and buying history to know what their buying habits are, so you can offer companion products or services to enhance their experience. Okay, so you've got this service, but if you wanted to upgrade or add something to it, it's going to help you even more. Right? You might want to recommend new and improved products or services that fit their needs as well. If there's a new version of a product that came out, let them know! You can see through their profile and buying history that they've got the old version, right? Send them an email, give them a phone call, or just let them know that this new product is out.

One of my favorites is watching movies online. You might watch a movie and think, "That was a pretty good movie." Then, when you look below the title screen, you may see a message that says, "Other people also watched these movies." I've found some great movies and TV shows that way. And you just click on it and there's this algorithm that says they are similar and other people watch them as well. Isn't that pretty cool? Now those companies are anticipating my future customer needs and that's all part of customer service. Make sense? Good.

Let's recap. Use your customer's profile and buying history to help anticipate their future needs. Offer companion products or services to enhance their experience, and recommend new and improved products and services that may fit their needs. If you do this, it is like the icing on the cake. This is going to really solidify that relationship, and you will get those customers who will never leave you. This is how you do it. This is how you provide something extra for your customers. See you guys in the next chapter.

Reflections on YOUR customer service:

What are three ways you can successfully anticipate what your customers will want from you and your company, and anticipate their future needs?

What is a possible positive outcome from anticipating your customer's future needs?

"It takes months to find a
customer . . . seconds to lose one."

—Vince Lombardi

CHAPTER 22

EVALUATING YOURSELF

In this chapter, we're going to continue with solutions. And this chapter has a little twist. This one involves you for you. What do I mean by that? You're going to evaluate the customer experience from your experience. Why is that important? Well, think about anybody who is the best in the world at what they do. Whether it's an athlete or an entertainer, or a CEO or a booming entrepreneur, they're constantly getting better, right? They're constantly looking for ways to improve themselves. And if you want to improve your revenues, if you want to increase the size of your paycheck, if you want advancement, if you want promotion, if you want to really deliver the best customer service, you have to continue to evolve.

How do you do that? One of the best ways is to ask yourself, after every transaction or every phone call or every customer that comes in the door, "Did I wow them and make the experience special?" And be honest with yourself, right? Because this is really about you. Did you wow them and make the experience special? If you did wow them, maybe jot it down. How did you do it? Keep a little journal or put it into your phone's notes or something. I did wow them, and this is what I did. And, if you didn't wow them, ask yourself, "On a scale from one to ten, how would I rate the customer's experience?" Right? Ask yourself: what could you have done to make the experience better, faster, friendlier, more fantastic? What could you have done? And maybe jot that down.

How does evaluating your own customer service help you continue to get better? Well, the next phone call, you can try these things. The next person that steps through the door, you'll be thinking about these things. And if you're doing this every day, day in and day out, you're asking, "Did I wow them and make the experience special? On a scale from one to ten, how would I rate that experience? What could I have done to make the experience better, faster, friendlier, more fantastic?" What's going to happen is you're going to start to see the things that work, and you're going to start to see the things that don't work. And you're going to start to get creative; it's going to really trigger that innovation in you, and you're going to think about how you could make things better. How you could make things different. When you ask yourself, "Gosh, what could I have done to make that a ten?" you will see an answer. Or, maybe you don't have the answer, so you'll go to a coworker or maybe you'll go to one of your leaders or team leads and ask them, "How would you suggest that I wow them and make their experience even more special?" Okay? And now you've got a collaborative effort as well. You're on the right track. But this is never ending. When does it end? Never. Improving customer service continues to go on and on. Just like top athletes—they're always pushing themselves to go a little faster, to go a little further, to be a little better. And they elevate themselves beyond their wildest dreams, and you can do that too in customer service. Don't settle for good when you can be fantastic. Enjoy the process of being the best, and whatever you do, don't quit challenging yourself to be a little better every day.

Reflections on YOUR customer service:

Why is it important for you to consistently get feedback on how well you are delivering excellent customer service?

What are three ways you can evaluate yourself after a customer service interaction?

"Information is king but only
when you act on it."

—David Brownlee

LAST WORDS

Congratulations! You just finished the book *Customer Service Success*. I hope you got great value from it. Now you have discovered the foundation for delivering excellent customer service, gaining loyalty, and making a positive difference in your business.

The question is, what's next? How do you implement what you've learned into your organization? The answer is easier than you might think.

I have taken all of the concepts, strategies, and blueprints from this book and put them into a brief, yet powerful, online training program for you and your staff. This program is a culmination of everything I've discovered over the last thirty years in customer service and customer success. The course is a series of videos, action guides and audio MP3s, so you can listen to the sessions on your phone or device anywhere you like; in the car, in your office, at your home, or even in the gym. You have 24/7 access, so you can watch videos or listen anytime. I'll be your instructor, and I know we'll have fun and learn a lot together. You'll also have access to our private community where you can ask questions, brainstorm, and share your successes with like-minded individuals and myself. Go to www.CustomerServiceSuccess.com and get started today for FREE!

I'm David Brownlee and thanks for allowing me to be your personal customer service and customer success coach. I'll see you soon in our community. You are a Rockstar!

ABOUT THE AUTHOR

David Brownlee is passionate about helping executives, business owners, and team members improve their customer success and customer service skills, so that they can achieve their goals faster, easier and with better results. David believes that we can each make a difference in someone's life for the better, one customer at a time.

David is the number one, best-selling author of *Rockstar Service, Rockstar Profits.* He is the CEO of The Pure Customer Service Training Company and an international speaker and trainer.

David has been in customer service and customer success for over thirty years and has trained over two million individuals and companies through his online courses, live events, and coaching programs. He has coached over five thousand one-on-one sessions with clients over the years, and he has delivered training in customer success and customer service to individuals from Google, LinkedIn, Amazon, Walmart, Microsoft, ATT, Citibank, CVS, T-Mobile, Hewlett-Packard, Harley-Davidson and others.

David currently lives in California, with his wife and two young children. When David isn't working or with family, you can find him on a motorcycle, scuba diving somewhere, or skiing down a mountain.

ALSO BY DAVID BROWNLEE

Rockstar Service, Rockstar Profits: Increase Your Revenues, Grow Your Business and Create Raving Fan Customers for Life

RockStar Service, Rockstar Profits reveals a new fast, easy way to increase revenues, grow a business, and create loyal customers for life.

Imagine for a moment that your favorite artist, musician, group or rock star came into your office or called you today requesting your product or service. What would you say to them? What would you do to serve them? Now ask yourself: When was the last time I treated a customer or a client like a rock star? What would it do for your business if you treat every customer and client like a rock star?

Rockstar Service, Rockstar Profits shows business owners, executives, customer service reps, and others a more effective way for their team to deliver world-class, Rockstar customer service to their customers. Inside, business coach David Brownlee teaches how to build rapport in 60 seconds or less, create customized customer service strategies to implement immediately, and how to look at customers in a new light. *Rockstar Service, Rockstar Profits* reveals how to increase revenues, grow a business, and create raving fans—clients that will never leave.

NOTES

★ ★ ★ ★ ★

NOTES

★ ★ ★ ★ ★

NOTES

★ ★ ★ ★ ★

NOTES

★ ★ ★ ★ ★

NOTES

★ ★ ★ ★ ★